Fields of Summer

Stephen Brooke

Arachis Press 2016

Will you taste July
with me? It promises
to be sweeter this year
than any I have known.

Fields of Summer
©2016 Stephen Brooke

ISBN 978-1-937745-35-6

Arachis Press
4803 Peanut Road
Graceville, FL 32440
http://arachispress.com

Fields of Summer

The air grew heavy with summer
and tomorrow slept in the fields,
dozing among the corn stalks
where cicadas sang

their tuneless lullaby.
There was, that season, a river
we could not cross, flooded
with our illusions. In stages

imperceptible,
it rose as we played
along its bowered banks,
at reckless dreams of love,

sun-lit games born in
the fervor and fever of spring.

And there was too much heat,
that summer, too many storms;
we were intoxicated
on secrets and the scent

of fresh-mown fields. We were
carried on the flood
of the river grown wide,
our banks undercut,

our sanctums swept away.
I have slept in those fields,
dreamed with tomorrow
of comings and of goings,

of the wind that turns
in its season. Of summer.

tomorrow slept in the fields

Open

Windows open
to the soft dusk,
I listen. Spring comes,
calling 'Chuck-Will's-Widow'
across the fields.

I heard this song
in the hollows
of my childhood.
I knew it as the voice
of first love,

tenuous, tender.
It is the song
of years past;
the light of fireflies
is in it.

FIELDS OF SUMMER

Greens

While the other seeds sleep
in a shoe-box, out in the garage,
the mustard goes into the ground.

Frost still paints the mornings
and those packets of anticipation
must wait. Not the greens;

they'll rise early to greet
a newly arrived Spring.
Wake up, gardener,

or you'll be left behind.

The Play

The drama in nine acts
plays again, on stages
from Fenway to barrio streets.

Each performance differs:
each actor finds his lines
written in the red stitching

of a fast ball conversation.
Give me the signs, again,
and I'll remember summer.

I'll remember the nights,
the high flies swarming up
into webs of light;

I'll return to the crowded
bleachers, lukewarm beer,
and long forgotten rookies

of every hot afternoon.
The play's the thing, you know;
it always has been.

FIELDS OF SUMMER

Beisbol

Down in Latin America, somewhere,
a kid eyes second base.

I don't know if he will take
that euphoric headlong rush,

but I wish I were there
to see it if he does.

Nest

Gather the unspoken words;
send them all to my heart.

There, they may hide themselves,
birds that need fly no further.

Let them rest, one season of storm;
Spring will call each to its home.

STEPHEN BROOKE

A Restless Season

Spring is a restless season,
a time for changes and beginnings,
for cleaning house, for planting garden.

A season for longing, a time to seek
new love, sprouting through the cracks
in our too long sleeping hearts.

How many times can we clean
an empty house, how often plant
to watch our garden wither

in Summer's heat? As many times
as Spring comes, my friends. Just as
many times as Spring comes.

FIELDS OF SUMMER

Strings

All the guitar strings
do not need to be changed
in Spring, but like the green
sprouts in the garden
they are a sign of new life,
the rebirth of a love
almost forgotten.
Will summer bring music
this year? I have pledged
it to myself
in bonds of bronze.

Spirals

Riding God's elevator
to the top floor,
the vulture is dark beauty
against the dry blue depths
of a spring sky.
She catches the sweet stench
of carrion and spirals
down, a falling angel.

STEPHEN BROOKE

Pear, in Blossom

The pear, come to full glorious stench
of beauty, throws herself at spring

before all other trees. She blooms
into the sky. A promise hangs

upon her branches, to bow with
all green-gold homage in their season,

as ripeness comes to she who now
will stand so modest in her white.

FIELDS OF SUMMER

Excess

She always did excess to excess
but that was the style, then.
Each needle hit the red-line.

Each song became the blues
as she tore pieces from
herself and scattered them.

She always went further and faster
toward nowhere than the rest of us.

STEPHEN BROOKE

Spring Cleaning

There is too much grass, too many
frogs and bugs and strands of weed
in the spring. It is a place
of life and growth and, sometimes, both
become a bit too exuberant.

This is my spring cleaning, whatever
the season, to scoop to a clean sand
bottom where I can fill my pails
with the clear cold water seeping
up through layers of sandstone and time.

The tadpoles will return but they
seek cover further down, now, where
the spring-born stream flows between
grassy, overhanging banks,
to find the creek and then away.

As I, too, carry away my share,
begrudged by neither Nature nor frogs.
There will be other days I make
my visit, bucket in either hand.
There will be other spring cleanings.

FIELDS OF SUMMER

Famous

I never met Bukowski but I know
this guy who knew him when and name-drops Hank
every now and again. He knew a lot
of famous dead guys back then, back in the Sixties,

and was kind of famous himself for a week
or two. I don't know if he'll ever live
that down but he keeps trying, looking for
the next comeback, getting straight for a while,

throwing away his damaged dream when doubt
taps him on the shoulder. But, hey, maybe
this time it will work; we do get older
and a little wiser, after all.

Older—there's the word we both fear now,
the has-been, the never-was. Better than being
dead, though, even dead and famous. Bukowski
will never write another poem.

STEPHEN BROOKE

In Tampa

The old women with their hennaed hair
remembered Havana. They had followed
husbands or fathers here, in the days
when cigar-making was the trade
in demand, the skill of the hand roll.

Before Castro, before even
Batista, the men had come and they
watched the beisbol games on the warm
Florida evenings and smoked
what they had created that day.

The fragrant salty bread from the corner
panaderia would remind them of home,
the cousins and brothers, and who
knew what had become of them when
revolution and time had broken their world.

And the old women were now the abuelas
and tias of a generation that did not
know Havana. They did not speak
Espanol or chose not to and danced
to the rock-and-roll with their girlfriends.

FIELDS OF SUMMER

That is the way things go, their children
tell them. We are Americans now.
On the park benches, the old women
with their flaming hair gossip of this
and much more and remember Havana.

Scrub Country

Carry me on the voice of crows;
I'll live the harsh music of your days,
hold the cicada heart of the evening,
the humming dusk, close to me.

Carry me to the pine-top sun;
a corvine shadow, I seek my name,
no more than a whispered sigh
of Spanish moss, a campfire song.

No more than the afternoon rain,
conversing with palmetto fronds—
Carry me on the voice of rivers;
I'll wear the heat of distant skies.

STEPHEN BROOKE

Falling

The sky is falling again;
the last time, I had stars
in my eyes and thought
I had fallen in love.

But no, only the sky
fell. Here's a piece
I kept—I think it fitted
near the moon in heaven's

jigsaw puzzle. I couldn't
put it back for she
would wax and wane and nothing
fitted anymore.

Let the stars stay put
tonight. I need clear eyes
if I am ever to put
my sky together again.

FIELDS OF SUMMER

The Gray Time

In the gray time
of bird calls and coffee,
in the hour of fading
dreams, the books take possession

of their shelves and the cat
and the other cat, gray and gray,
dance to me, and day
must begin here. Across

the dawn, I seek my words,
sometimes waiting at the tip
of a number two pencil,
sometimes as elusive

as the dew's conversations
with the grass, in this time,
the gray time
of beginning.

STEPHEN BROOKE

Seeds

I have saved your every word;
kept each for planting in my fields.

Now, they lie fallow; these seeds will sleep.
But in its season, all that passed

between us will be trained upon
an arbor framed of verse, a vine

gravid with our ripened fruit.
I will bottle you like wine.

FIELDS OF SUMMER

Canary

The canary does not sing in summer;
busy growing a new yellow suit,
he lacks the energy.
When it's ready, he'll call

for females to admire him,
with all his fine color on display,
a song of warning
to imaginary rivals.

He'll be the bird I first saw
singing in a tiny cage.

Come, Join Me

Come, join me, love, your melody
will find in me its harmony;
your instrument I'll gladly be
as I play you and you play me.

Come, join me, love, beneath the moon,
come share with me your secret tune;
allow our music rise and soon
as one voice will our hearts commune,

and as it surges it will seem
that all past sorrow be but dream.
Come, join me, love, we'll craft a theme
of cricket chorus and moonbeam,

to hold all that for which we long;
come, join me, love, in this our song.

FIELDS OF SUMMER

Your Name

These sultry nights, as spring
awakens into summer,
I breathe the violet air
of you. Some subtle breeze
has borne your essence here,
whispering, whispering your name.

Among the moon-cast shadows
dance fire-flies; can my heart
yet solve the mysteries
of night's elusive song?
It whispers, whispers your name.

avoid those shadowed pools

FIELDS OF SUMMER

Those Pools

There are leeches in the creek.
If you stay out here where the sun
shines through to bottom it will be okay.
Just avoid those shadowed pools.

Even on a hot July day,
the water is too cold to go
seeking shade, back under the boughs
of overhanging hemlocks, dark

with the mysteries of forest. Stay here
by me on this gravel spit,
where the water laughs at the sun
and runs away in little ripples

down into its stillness of pools.
There are leeches in those pools.

Storm

The gentlest of breezes signals
the approach of the tempest.

Viridian pines sway on the hills
dancing to the wind's wild song.

The air is alive with the scent
of our electricity.

Drifting

Drifting into you, after
all these years: I, the cautious
one, fearful of who I am
and of who you think I am

or might become. Eyes closed,
I could have run to you. Eyes closed,
drifting into fitful night,
I've often prayed I would not waken

FIELDS OF SUMMER

and you, who never heard my words,
will not now deny me this
awakening nor this drifting,
my slow drifting into you.

Alleluia

It is the time of hurting,
that harvest we always knew
must follow such a planting—
beneath the first full moon
of Spring, our crop was sown.
No matter, no matter; you must
hurt me as I will you,
for giving and forgiving
have their parts. Each dawn
whispers of the day
to come, our redemption.
Each dawn sings alleluia.

STEPHEN BROOKE

The Pillow

It couldn't be resisted, I suppose,
even sitting up high where she had
to jump to reach it. I've placed pillows
there before, on the brick plinths

supporting the weathered columns.
One day I'll have to replace those
or the porch roof will be coming down
on me. It's a good place to set things

though, to dry or to air. The pillows do get
wet; it's part of my daily routine, the damp
bedding and clothes, the rinsing and refreshing.
What is that to a playful dog? I'd put it high

but she can jump high. It's part of the game,
reach what one can, tear it apart, never mind
the rebukes that will follow. She knows
I'll love her again soon. I always do.

FIELDS OF SUMMER

Briefcase

This battered briefcase holds my name
and my heart, locked away
with papers of long-concluded business,
their illegible signatures giving

witness to yesterday's sworn truths.
I misplaced the key some time ago
but is easy to carry and so
shabby none would think to steal it.

I remember how the hinges
creaked the last time it was opened,
and that the leather is only plastic.
I remember filling it

with the sugar sand of our beach
and the cloud you said looked like
a hippopotamus but then
it turned into a cat before

becoming nothing, nothing at all.
Who knows what it might be now;
that transaction lies between
the notarized pages and empty folders.

The case can not be opened without
breaking the catches. Where then would I
keep my heart, my name? Must I file them
away with other finished business

in cardboard boxes labeled year
by year until they now longer matter?
I'll carry this briefcase to yet another
meeting, as if I had a key.

FIELDS OF SUMMER

Pratfall

The apprentice clown has learned
all his master's tricks,

save one. He can fall
but not yet pick himself up,

laughing with the crowd.
They still see the pain,

hide it though he does
behind greasepaint and wig.

They see him wince, and know
the cost of each pratfall.

STEPHEN BROOKE

In Vino Veritas

The focaccia is just out of the oven
and I've a bottle of Bardolino uncorked
and whispering its secrets into the spare room's
darkened air. There is basil and thyme

in the crust, the richness of olives ripened
by the Mediterranean sun. No rosemary,
though; I know you don't like the rosemary.
Come, sit here by the window and I'll cut

the bread while you pour wine. There is truth
in wine, remember, so fill my glass and I'll
say things to regret later. But that
will be too late, won't it? No matter;

I'd regret not saying them as well.

FIELDS OF SUMMER

Clarity

The clarity of moonlight was the subject
and whether the trees spoke more freely
at night. I claimed it to be so
but you doubted. Oh, we have discussed you

often, I and the moon and the trees.
They tell me you hide from them,
that you are deaf and blind.
Listen. The pine keeps no secrets.

Luna shows her face to lovers
and to the lost. Let her lead you
to my arms. Give the trees your song,
in the clarity of moonlight.

Tonight

Tonight, we will wear
our love and nothing more.
Let tomorrow bring
its fashions, it colors;
the sun loves all new things.
But tonight, I am clothed
in you and you in me.

Tonight, I must love you.
It is the time for us;
later, we may read the sky
and find new essence
in our stars. They have shone
us the way here. Might they
not whisper to what end, tonight?

FIELDS OF SUMMER

Through the Night
a ghazal

The south wind carries my gift through the night;
The flight of love is swift through the night.

In the dark, we sing each other to sleep,
Our lullabies adrift through the night.

The breeze that bears my lover's voice blows steady;
I pray it does not shift through the night.

Many are the songs that speak your name
A Lad's lone voice will lift through the night.

Shards

The current of who I am
undercuts my life,
carries me away
piece by piece.
Gather me.
Gather up those bits
left smooth by the flood
and sell them in the market.
Gather up the shards
that can never be whole
again, to place on your mantel.
I will sing there
all the long nights.

Indicative

Indicative of nothing,
I gather up a handful
of your seasons in brown
and orange and broken

FIELDS OF SUMMER

pieces of themselves.
Flung across holiday tables,
they were. Sit here, by me,
ladies, one on either side.

Flung across Christmas
and Easter, they were,
and caught in gauze.
Yes, the blonde to my right,

you with the darkness spilling,
at my left. Or the other
way round, if you wish.
It is, as always,

indicative of nothing.
So speak not; you said
quite enough before
and put a period on it.

Into garages you sent
your words, into kitchens;
into hesitant rooms
indicative of nothing.

Morning Song

The cardinal is first; then mockingbirds join
and sometimes a distant titmouse. It is gray
yet, outside, and the fog sleeps on the fields.
Soon every bird will join to sing the sun
into the summer sky and me from my bed.

Some close windows to keep out the night
but they also keep out the new day;
I would fall asleep to the chuck-will-widow's
lullaby and waken to the cardinal's whistle,
the wren's rustling at my sill.

There is a stillness of the air in this hour,
no breeze upon the fields nor business
of insects. Dawn will burn away
the fogs that cling to summer's edge;
winds will rise to finish morning's song.

FIELDS OF SUMMER

The Song

In caverns known but to the tides,
the blind fish turn their silvered sides;
beneath a phosphorescent moon,
they dance the ageless murmured tune

of sea and earth and hidden places.
A song, in turn, each drop that traces
its path along the dew-wet blade
of lawn takes up, lets rise and fade,

and, whispered by the rains of night,
the melody lifts into flight,
as wind gives music subtle wings,
to fill the dark between all things.

STEPHEN BROOKE

These Hills

These hills are older than you and I.
They're older than our fathers and mothers
and their fathers and mothers and the tribes
that left their broken pots and arrowheads

in the caves and in the fields.
I've found them there in new-plowed soil
by the creek, like the grains of corn
left from long-ago failed harvests.

These hills were young when the world was young.
Their sandstone skeleton hardened an aeon
before the dinosaurs crossed over them.
They were mountains, then, sky-touched

heights, sheer cliffs of golden sunlight.
That sun's vigor we'll not know again.
These hills are old now, soft rounded remnants
crumbling into gentle oblivion.

FIELDS OF SUMMER

These forest-covered hills of home,
these hills of abandoned orchard and field,
of secluded hollow and cave,
dream the dreams of ages past

and you and I and our sons and daughters
will be as the arrowheads in the field.

Background

The rhythm of tonight
pulses dark and slow
as an adagio
of cricket violins
fades into the background
of us.

STEPHEN BROOKE

Pine Cones

All night, I lobbed pine cones at the moon,
hoping to dislodge it from the sky.

You held a jar ready so you might carry it home,
place it by the bed to light our lovemaking.

We should have been there rather than staring upward
at the slow transit of the heavens.

A Song for Tomorrow

Tomorrow is a song I wrote for you.
To whom should I now sing? The tune is lost;
it echoes in my deserts, empty places
between desire and the waning moon.

Bring me my guitar, a glass of wine,
and yesterday will find its melody.
I'll fill this night with stars a while, forgetting
I have no song, no music for tomorrow.

FIELDS OF SUMMER

Fog

Still dark. Fog slept on the fields,
in layered blankets of silence.

She watched his taillights dissolve into
the morning and turned from the window.

'Stay, next time,' she whispered. 'Stay.'
Miles away, he turned on the radio.

Beat

Drum on me. The sound will fill
all tonight and overflow
across the morning as two hearts
find polyrhythmic accord, a beat
to echo against those unnamed stars,
newly risen at our first kiss.

Sweeter

My sister offered the use
of a tiller but I,
being old-school, prefer
a shovel, a rake, my hands.

I'll not be hurried; the garden
and I will take our time,
finding the way to summer
along these new-sprung roads.

Will you taste July
with me? It promises
to be sweeter this year
than any I have known.

FIELDS OF SUMMER

That Summer

That summer of seduction,
we were young and in love
with ourselves, with

the lovers we had become.
We followed a script we would write,
scene by scene, each day.

There was nothing new
in that story, yet
each cliche held wonder

for us, a discovery
of us as we would dream
we were. And so we were,

for a season, a summer;
we filled our eyes with stars
and the night sky whispered

fresh lines for our play.
We learned them well, you and I,
eager to speak them, eager

to play the roles we'd chosen,
to be young lovers, all
that summer of seduction.

Apples

You handed me my first Braeburn
that evening, while Jim Billie played,
and maybe that is why it tasted
better than any apple I'd bit
into before, with all the flavor
of our love and a warm May night.
Each since tastes of those memories,
grown sweeter with the ripening
of six seasons' insistent passage:
you and May and the music of apples
and fireflies dancing among the pines.

FIELDS OF SUMMER

Crescent

A dark beauty fills the hungry arms
of the crescent moon.

They have joined, becoming one light,
as each completes the other.

I have dreamed, oh yes, dreamed of you
fitted to the curve of me.

Bring

Bring me the light of fireflies,
the cobweb's thread, and I
shall fashion a gown of night for you.

Bring me the evening breeze
and I shall set it whispering
all my secrets in your ear.

And bring me your kiss, your draught
of stars, that I might deeply
drink and never thirst till dawn.

when summer sings anew

FIELDS OF SUMMER

Weather

Graphite slabs of storm
rumbled their way from the south.
We breathed in the cool electricity
of our love. In nervous cages,
the doves fell silent;
your dogs huddled at our bare feet.
Did I kiss you then? I think
so. Or was it only
insistent rain making love
to the roof?

You filled those afternoons,
now further from me,
and poured them into
the softness of the night.
What stars burnt through, as we
wore each other's words!
Now, I slip into someone
else's. The fit of yours
grew loose; they fell
from me at season's end.

What storms divide us
when summer sings anew?
Your gift of clouds
lifts white hands to beg
my time. I have none.
Only the rains of memory
remain with me, climbing
a sullen southern sky.
Do you wear the weather
well, this year?

We Both

We both had too much wine that night
and talked for hours of food,

how we might open a restaurant.
We knew we never would.

We both were still in love that night.
I reached across the table

to take your hand for just a moment.
The moment passed too soon.

FIELDS OF SUMMER

The Last Party

Scattered plastic chairs,
their plainness turned
to ruddy chiaroscuro
by the dying bonfire,

lay dark paths upon her lawn,
her fresh-mown fragrant lawn,
beneath summer's stars.
Couple by lingering couple,

our guests hugged and farewelled
and welcomed me to the family
before flipping on headlights
and driving out of my life.

In the silent
emptiness of then,
I held her to me,
both of us too exhausted,

both a little too full
of Sam Adams—
her brother had brought
a keg— to make love

that July night,
three weeks before
we said goodbye.

Dove

The heart is a dove;
throw it to the sky,
let it fly home
on eager wings.

It remembers the way.
Tomorrow, you may
find it asleep
in its nest of dream.

FIELDS OF SUMMER

This Place

I have designed this place
and built it from scraps of desire,
the leftover ends of dreams.
It stands on its shadow
in desert depths.
It floats on the jungled rains.
And always, the doors open
into those rooms
I meant for you.

Ashes, ashes,
it all falls down.

I burn it to your memory
and each tomorrow
find myself rebuilding.
Shall I set it ablaze
once again,
allow the merciful flames
to consume this place,
this house of ashes
I meant for you?

Genesis

I was temptation, the very fruit
your father had forbidden you.
Who, then, played the snake in Eden?
Single minded, simple minded,
I could not see that, also, was I,
hissing songs only I understood.

Once, swift angels of your gate
knew me as friend; they have flown
away with all my keys, no longer
bearing swords nor baring teeth.
What need when I exiled myself
so thoroughly from Paradise?

I shall remain a wanderer,
driven from the gates of dawn,
the rising sun of your farewell kiss.
This garden, grown as guarded as I,
is closed to me and to my heart's
children for all their generations.

FIELDS OF SUMMER

A House of Cards

I placed each card,
building higher day by day,
and every time it shook
so did my heart.

Should I have been surprised
when it all came down?
Should it have hurt the less?

I will not build such houses
for a while;
but, in time, I'll stack

more cards, one atop another.
I'll try to build to heaven
once again.

STEPHEN BROOKE

The Woman Who Made Me a Poet

Unaware, the woman
who made me a poet
goes about her days

in a house full of dogs.
Different dogs, now,
than those that crowded us

on the couch and I
do not know their names.
Not that it matters. I have

words now, sleeping at
my side, fetching memories
I toss upon the green

lawns of years ago.
And the woman who made
me a poet does not

know these games; she does
not know these words that found
their way to my door,

tails wagging, begging to be
taken in. She does
not know they speak of her.

Two Miles

There's a rest stop up ahead, two miles,
and I've driven all the hours of dark.
'How far is too far?' asks the night. 'How far?'

Does each exit ramp lead to another
heart, a heart that yearned along this highway?
I find no music on the radio.

Pull over here and nap. It's almost dawn
and only one more hour to her. 'How far
is too far?' I ask the night. 'How far?'

STEPHEN BROOKE

Your Portrait

Your portrait became my farewell; we all have our ways
of saying goodbye to those we loved and perhaps
love still. Did you know your half-finished likeness sat staring
from the easel when you chose to go?
My surprise, the one anniversary gift
my heart could afford. I ripped it into the tattered
useless scraps of canvas it had already
become for me. Yet your face remained unfinished
business; only the exorcism of paint
would banish it from my dreams. And from my dreams
came truth, in ochre and cerulean
and all the tones of the love we shared. Keep it—
I painted it for you.
I painted it for me.

FIELDS OF SUMMER

Now and Then

Do I make you crazy? you'd ask now and then,
over some small silly thing you might do.
No, kid, I'd tell you, and smile. It was true,
oh, it was so true, when you'd ask, now and then.

And did you at last, or was it that I knew
my teetering dance on the tight rope of you
could only end with a fall? Who made who
mad is a question I ask, now and then.

Only

Only time can walk through that door
into the overgrown jungles of your
gardened heart. Only light
can be hidden by light, and night

can only hide itself in night.
Give me your liana hand,
green as grasshoppers, green as Oz,
and wrap yourself around tomorrow.

STEPHEN BROOKE

Only time can find its way,
machete-hacking its path to cities
of emerald and gold. It sings
as it works, swinging, swinging,

to tunes from a tinny radio.
They made those in Japan, when I
was a kid. Time carried them all
off to China and my evenings

followed, swinging a baseball bat,
swinging for the fences, the hidden
night that waits above the lights.
Only time can catch that ball.

FIELDS OF SUMMER

To Memory

Do I miss her? Oh sure,
sometimes. Those were
the best and worst of times,
a Dickens of a time.

She wouldn't get that
and there it is. That was
the divide I could never
cross, no matter how high

we flew. Hell, yes, I miss her.
I miss her when fireflies
spell our names in the hollows
of a soft Spring night.

Uncork the wine; I'll drink
my solitary toast to memory

Painted

We walked hand in hand through the art show,
creating portraits of each other.

Memories are painted in the vivid hues
of cobalt and alizarin.

It has been long since we were in love
but not long enough for them to fade.

A Sad Song

She has become
a sad song I once heard—
words now half-forgotten
yet the melody lingers.

At times, I lie awake,
that tune filling the night,
and try to remember.
It fades, it fades.

FIELDS OF SUMMER

Book of Days

My book of days you are,
the pages of my life,
limned in leaf of gold
and lapis lazuli.

In you, I'll read my matins,
my prayers at none and vespers.
In you, my sun shall rise;
you'll be my evening star.

My book of days you are,
my comings and my goings,
the planting and the harvest,
each sorrow, every joy.

And all the seasons pass,
I'll read anew the year;
my book you are until
I close my eyes and sleep.

Yearn

The shadow you cast
has outlasted
the memory of our sun.
It shone on your face.

We made the dawn
our lover, then;
we slept in the cool arms
of a summer past.

Night and all
its distant stars
tell me I once dreamed,
and dreams must slip away.

Would I were
a pine, binding
rock-rooted earth to sky.
I yearn toward heaven.

FIELDS OF SUMMER

Kettle

The kettle has boiled dry.
For a time, it sang

my cheerful tune, whistled
of love and hot tea and you.

For a time, there was comfort
on these nights of rain.

It has a voice no longer.
The fire has left it empty.

Somewhere

Everywhere is on the road
to somewhere else, another town,
another love. I've tried to tarry
but someone always says, *Move on.*

This is not the place for you.
Someone says, *Tomorrow waits*
further along, around the bend.
I can smell the pines, growing

close and dark beside the road.
Let me lay my head here just
a little while, breathing in
the songs they have remembered, left

by the wind before it, too,
traveled on to somewhere else.

FIELDS OF SUMMER

Rain Day

Morning speaks of storms,
not with the red sky of warning—
or is that gray?

Ask a sailor.

Announced with distant thunder,
the day builds tumultuous towers,
walls of rain.

That's warning enough.

The dogs, cowed by the rumble,
take refuge in the closet,
the master walk-in.

It's their safe room.

Muffled rooftop drums—
a crescendo comes on
lightning cymbals.

They fade from me

to a tuneless murmur.
Once, I would hear words
on the wind.

Should I have answered?

Misted windows open
on misted skies, awash
in memories

of other rains.

Such days cross the horizon,
days of gray ennui
and misplaced time.

We'll find it tomorrow.

FIELDS OF SUMMER

Crates

I have placed yesterday on sale,
half-priced until we close. After
that, it goes into the dumpster

with the wilted lettuce and moldy
cheese. Let the homeless root
about and take the broken pieces.

I have no use for them. Crates
of tomorrow already wait
to be unloaded and placed on shelves.

STEPHEN BROOKE

Wax

Which moon rises? Wane the more
so I might wax into you.

My poems have put on paper slippers
and seek you past the unnamed stars.

We will be the dark, spilling
across a night that lives between us.

I leave my name at the door,
to enter you as a new man.

FIELDS OF SUMMER

Crumbs

We set a feast, pour the wine,
at this table of our past
but neither reaches for his goblet
nor tastes of the main course, for fear
that all we have laid out grows cold.
Shall we starve together this night?
It has been too long since I
fed on your lips. Each memoried kiss
seems less filling, less substantial,
the stale crumbs I would brush away
if I did not so hunger. The silence
remains untasted on my plate.

STEPHEN BROOKE

Miracle

Love was once another color,
a deeper color. The suns and storms
of summer faded it, incessant
in their song of murmured rain.

I remember the richness of lawns
so green I would have set them shining
against the topaz morning and strung
a necklace of endless day for you.

You scoffed when I sought miracles
in each new day, along our path
from here to there, to our sunset.
Yes, I call it miracle.

A miracle must be in the eye
of the beholder. Its origin
matters not, only its meaning.
What meaning has a morning, now?

FIELDS OF SUMMER

It has become the stuff of old
books, a wonder written down
for those who will believe. I can
no longer claim it as my own.

What Then?

Had I protested your leaving, what then?
Might you have stayed for a week, for a month?
Had I protested that I loved you still,
it would have ended the same.

Better by far that our love did not linger,
withering season by season of doubt.
Better that memory sing of our summer
that never led to a fall.

STEPHEN BROOKE

Piano

What song is that the rain
plays on the window glass?
A long untuned piano
plinks random notes against
orchestral thunder.

Tell me again of love
and all it promises;
tell me who writes such empty
concertos of the night.
I'll listen this time

and try to understand
its nuanced rhythms yet.
Then maybe we can dance
our uncertain tango
when next it rains.

FIELDS OF SUMMER

I Lost the Day

I lost the day,
cloud by cloud;

my minutes washed away
in unspoken showers.

In reluctant rains,
I cover my tomorrow;

you will not see me there,
across the lamp-lit ways,

across those streets
where I lost the day.

STEPHEN BROOKE

Remembered Sky

We've seen the setting sun before.
Let it go; this night, too,
will pass across the painted
horizons of our memory.

But listen! The morning star may whisper
our names, even as she fades.
Then leave your heart open
to the dawn, to the wounds of my kisses

and the healing of my embrace.
The glare of day hides every scar;
every star we know
must live in our remembered sky.

FIELDS OF SUMMER

Fading

Yesterday was a song
of heat and rain
but each morning now

the sun calls my name
a little later, a little
less insistently,

and seasons spin
about the North Star,
God's bull-roarer humming.

Tomorrow's tune will
carry a cold cadence,
a discord of winds,

but I still hear Summer
fading in the mornings,
gently fading away.

Flow

The slowly flowing ichor of these hours
fills me, chokes my veins, and all ambition
sleeps, lulled by subdued and subtle rhythms
of heat, insistent wordless songs of night.

Rain whispers at the glass, reminding me
of each promise life once made. Tomorrow,
they may lie forgotten, to be tripped
upon and cursed, debris of some time past,

and day will slowly flow from the horizon.

FIELDS OF SUMMER

Dirt

To move a barrow or two
of earth is no great deal;
shovel it in here,
dump it over there,
wipe the grit from your brow.

The sun will be high soon—
a barrow or two of dirt,
that's all, and then the cool
satisfaction of lemons
and ice and kitchen chairs.

Calendar

The calendar is two months off,
unflipped pages reminding me

of how little time matters as day
follows nameless day. The sun

rose this morning and it will
rise tomorrow and August can call

itself June. I like the picture
for this month. I'll look at it

a while longer and maybe let
September be June, too. Why not?

FIELDS OF SUMMER

Wrens

A wren hunts all around the window
frame, clinging, creeping,
poking into spider webs
I should have cleared away

last year or the year before.
They'll probably remain
next year, also, noticed only
now and then or never.

There are no longer plans drawn up,
lists written and rewritten.
Each day is like the last and I
don't know if it is Monday

or tomorrow. The sun does not
care, the rain still falls,
and being alone is almost as bad
as being with someone else.

The days flit, brown as wrens, seeking
and singing and building nests,
as seasons pass, and night speaks
of owls until I sleep.

Wine

The wine was bad. Not gone-sour bad
nor oxidized bad but simply cheap-swill bad.
I love good wine; I'll tolerate bad wine.

My reflection floated in the glass.
Floating somewhere in the back of my mind
was the question whether I would be

educating yet another love
in the ways of the vine. God knows, there was
little else I could teach anyone.

She leaned over to kiss and refill me.

FIELDS OF SUMMER

What I Have Lost

I could not hold my memories;
though time may lessen all our sorrows,
I did not wish them to so slip
between my fingers into that
dark flow of the forgotten.

Let me build a boat of words,
let me pursue what I have lost
around the curve of yesterday.
It will be there, lodged among
the rocks, what I have lost.

STEPHEN BROOKE

Nothing Matters

Nothing matters, I tell myself
as many times a day as needed,
like taking aspirin each four hours
for the chronic pain of life.

Nothing matters, I say, and it
is or isn't true and that
doesn't matter either, does it?
A mantra of indifference weaves

the hours together, pages of
my daily office, read in duty
and allowed to pass. Tomorrow will be
and I murmur, *nothing matters*.

FIELDS OF SUMMER

In Rain

The weariness of morning comes
in rain, sweeping night's remnants
into clear cold rivers. Whose name
do the doves whisper? They speak
of you, call you back to me,

among the shadows of the dawn.
In rooms removed, your piano
speaks languages I'll never learn.
I strain to find the meaning in these
conversations with forgotten

Russians, as day runs down the windows.
I'll take my solace by the cup,
dark coffee grown on green Andean
slopes of distance, and find myself
humming your half-remembered tunes.

soil and soul shall rest a season

FIELDS OF SUMMER

Fallow

For a season, this, my field,
must lie fallow. Year to year,

I have seen its yield diminish,
yesterday's sweet memories

fade to sere reality.
Once I knew a vigor here,

in the fertile, fruitful soil
of my youth. What harvests grew—

truths sprang singing from that earth,
plucked fresh, savored. We devoured

summers past, the ripened days
bursting with their golden promise.

We, too, ripened in that time,
tasted of the sun, embraced

night's soft rains. The breezes whispered
subtle, honey-scented secrets,

rising as the moon and stars
slowly turned on heaven's wheel,

even as we rose and fell
toward tomorrow. All now fails

in me; our past is the dust
borne on a relentless wind.

This day has no words, no color;
I grow meager as my crops,

fitful as these dreams of you.
What was spent would be repaid—

field and man must sometime sleep,
heal and wake to bloom once more.

Soil and soul shall rest a season;
this, my field, now must lie fallow.

FIELDS OF SUMMER

Cooling

Open the windows. These days are cooling
like the loaf of bread, fresh-baked,
resting, waiting, on my counter.

It's cool enough to bake the brown,
fragrant loaves of whole wheat bread,
yeasty, moist beneath the crust,

and scones, full of butter and raisins
and lemon zest. Autumn follows
summer's oven; the year is cooling,

cooling, and soon we will feast.

STEPHEN BROOKE

Fashion

It was with care I put
my happiness away, there
on the top shelf. Maybe

someday I can get it down,
unfold it, smooth the wrinkles
and see if it still fits.

It used to be all the fashion.

Jar

The days become
a jar full of pennies
to count out on the table,
fifty to the stack.

Oh, here's an old wheat,
real copper. They don't
make those, any more.
No, not any more.

FIELDS OF SUMMER

Let's put it in
another jar, a jar full
of yesterday's pennies
and roll the rest of these.

Colors

The colors of summer,
of grasshoppers and of rain
and of every rocket that climbed
the skies of July—
I gathered them for you
to burn in Autumn's bonfires.

Tomorrow, they are smoke
and ashes, hanging in the still air,
cold and colorless as the morning
of the first freeze.

Travelers All

Travelers all, we wear
the dust of yesterday.

The rain will fall at last,
gently wash away

each fragment of the past,
the long road's clinging clay.

Travelers all, we fare
yet upon our way.

Taste

I have hungered for my slice
of forever, one small piece.

Taste eternity with me;
we shall savor it until

all the stars grow dim and fail
and God calls creation home.

FIELDS OF SUMMER

Magnolia

The last magnolia petals float
upon the breath of summer.

They have become the scraps of paper
that bore your farewell message.

Blossoms return in their season;
will love ever bloom again?

Mist

Paintings of mist and songs of regret
always find an audience,
seeking, straining, to decipher
the whispers of the morning, dreams
that dissipate before the sun.

I can not tell what hides within
the shifting colors of my dawn,
but each brush stroke, every word,
assures me there are truths obscured,
secrets we misplaced last night.

Are those best forgotten, left
shapeless in the fog? The tunes
can still be hummed, those to which
we danced that yesterday, and each
daub of gray holds yet some color.

The Stars

I know how far it is to the stars.
They put that sort of thing in books
and I can say that point of light
that shines over there is such a distance
and that one is a little more,
a trillion miles or so. A trifle.

What is a star but light? That light
is with us now, each star set in
tonight's vast sky, their distance the same,
each casting faint star-shadows on
our world. Forget what books might say;
we hold the stars. We always have.

FIELDS OF SUMMER

Leaves

Each day now carries
its message of change,
written on a falling leaf
or a frosted window.

Autumn speaks with the voice
of birds in fervent flight,
wings spread upon
the faith of October.

The wind-tossed leaf—
does it too yearn
to seek a land
of eternal summer?

We can follow
only a little way,
the leaves and I;
only a little way.

STEPHEN BROOKE

Inventory

You needn't have worried;
I just stepped out
to count the stars.

I thought I heard
them falling, falling,
falling all night

like summer rain.
Sleep, my love,
sleep on; I've taken

my inventory
and all is well
above and below.

Fields of Summer is the fifth collection of adult poetry and nineteenth book from the pen of Stephen Brooke. For more of his writing, including novels and children's books, please visit the Arachis Press. http://arachispress.com

The text of his book is set in Sorts Mill Goudy, by Barry Schwartz